CONDUCTING
BASIC AND ADVANCED
SEARCHES

JASON PORTERFIELD

rosen publishing's
rosen
central®

New York

Published in 2010 by The Rosen Publishing Group, Inc.
29 East 21st Street, New York, NY 10010

Library of Congress Cataloging-in-Publication Data

Porterfield, Jason.
Conducting basic and advanced searches / Jason Porterfield.—1st ed.
    p. cm.—(Digital and information literacy)
Includes bibliographical references and index.
ISBN-13: 978-1-4358-5316-4 (library binding)
1. Internet searching—Juvenile literature. 2. Web search engines—Juvenile literature.
3. Computer network resources—Evaluation—Juvenile literature. I. Title.
ZA4230.P67 2010
025.0425—dc22

2008046783

Manufactured in Malaysia

CONTENTS

INTRODUCTION

For many people, it may be hard to imagine life without the Internet. People use the World Wide Web to communicate, play games, and gather news. Many also go on the Internet to search for information using search engines. In fact, some sources say that searching is the second-most popular use of the Internet behind e-mail.

However, the flood of information available online can seem overwhelming. Today, billions of Web pages are available on the World Wide Web. While anyone with Internet access can technically look at any of the Web's many sites, the thought of sorting through all of the possibilities for specific information may be intimidating, particularly to new users. Even for experienced users, the amount of information available through the Internet may seem overwhelming unless a user knows a specific Web address—called a URL, short for "uniform resource locator"—or uses a search engine.

Search engines can be defined simply as major Web sites capable of directing Internet users to different Web pages and access points like directories and community sites at the same time. The earliest search engines were designed to help users search the Web by specific topics.

Search engines may return a wide variety of sites. These can include general Web documents based on data gathered by the search engine.

They can also include subject directories that have been listed at the request of Web site creators or results from companies and individuals that have paid to have their Web site listed among returns. Some returns may be data screened by people, screened automatically by computer programs based on the popularity of certain sites, and data automatically uploaded from online publications like newspapers, magazines, and journals.

Chapter 1

Search Engine Basics

Search engines are basically massive databases, not unlike the card catalog in a library. While a single search may bring up hundreds, thousands, or even millions of results, search engines do not actually search the entire Internet. They search only Web pages and sites that already have been categorized and stored by the search engine.

While each search engine may work differently, they are all made up of three basic elements: a crawler, an indexer, and the query process.

Crawlers

Crawlers—sometimes called spiders, robots, or worms—are computer programs that visit Web pages, download all of the information on those pages, and then follow links to other pages within the Web site. They then send this information on to the search engine's indexer.

There are two ways that crawlers find information. In the early days of the Internet, people could add their sites to search engine databases.

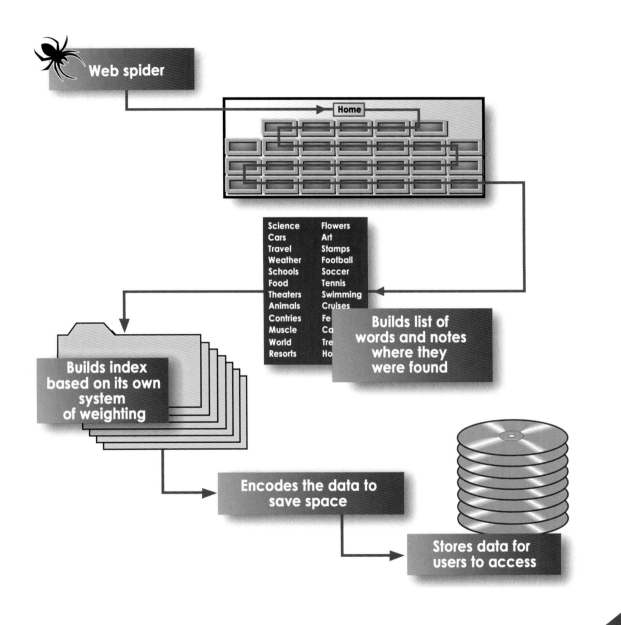

Web spider

Home

Science   Flowers
Cars   Art
Travel   Stamps
Weather   Football
Schools   Soccer
Food   Tennis
Theaters   Swimming
Animals   Cruises
Contries   Fe
Muscle   Ca
World   Tre
Resorts   Ho

Builds list of
words and notes
where they
were found

Builds index
based on its own
system
of weighting

Encodes the data to
save space

Stores data for
users to access

Web crawlers, often called spiders, follow patterns to find information on the Web and then
store this information to make it easier for search engines to find.

Unfortunately, some users abused this method by sending fake posts, forcing search engine companies to phase out that method of notification. Today, crawlers look at the URL links on Web pages automatically and then review them to screen out any bogus links.

Along with analyzing and indexing information, the crawler makes other refinements to the information it gathers before it becomes available to Internet users. Crawlers detect and remove spam pages (pages that falsely feature search terms in order to get users to visit them), find and delete duplicate pages, and also do some quality testing on search terms and results. All of this makes crawling the Internet very expensive for search companies, so most set a limit on the number of pages on a Web site that a crawler may visit. These Web sites remain un-indexed, and while the potentially valuable information on them is still available to users, it is harder to find than indexed information.

The time that it takes for crawlers to index Web pages can be a drawback to using search engines to find up-to-date information. Some crawlers can index millions of Web pages a day, but the vast size of the Internet sometimes causes delays between the time information goes up on the Web and the time that a crawler finds it. Many search engine companies claim that their crawlers are constantly looking for the most recent information available, but some studies have shown that these companies are often weeks behind in re-crawling and indexing material.

Indexers

The indexer is the part of the search engine that collects, classifies, and categorizes all of the information the crawler finds. Until a search engine indexes a Web page, that page remains unavailable to people using the search engine. Once the Web page is indexed, any changes that are later made to the Web page are updated in the index so that the changes can be reflected in searches.

A Web page is logged and then stored in the search engine's database by the indexer. This allows the search engine to expand its search beyond keyword searches and find words that are close to each other, usually through the advanced search options offered by many search engines. Some search engines also index the coding of Web sites, enabling the search engine to look by using Web page categories, such as titles or even URLs.

The indexing is done by a software program, and indexers use mathematical formulas to calculate the rankings of returns for the search terms entered. Many indexers eliminate common words that do not impact search results, such as "and," "for," and "is," from the search engine's database to make the search engine perform more efficiently. Some search engine indexers also eliminate punctuation marks and change letters to make the search engine work faster.

Other Prominent Search Engines

Since the Internet became available for public use, hundreds of search engines have been created. Many more have either been discontinued or absorbed by larger companies or remain obscure. Others have existed for years.

The search engine AltaVista has been around since 1995, though it has been owned by parent company Overture since 2003. AltaVista is easy to use, fast, and large. Its advanced search options allow users to perform very precise searches through phrase searches, by highlighting keywords, and even by using case-sensitive matches to find words with upper-case letters.

Yahoo! began in 1994 as a directory, which categorizes information rather than searches for it, and now uses its own crawler to perform searches. Yahoo! allows searches in other languages and returns results that include maps and images. Yahoo! has a sizable list of shortcuts that allow users to quickly find data ranging from local temperatures to driving directions.

Live Search is a search site owned and operated by software giant Microsoft. Live Search offers several innovative features, such as allowing users to scroll through additional search results on the same page rather than having to keep clicking on pages to see results. The search engine also allows users to adjust the amount of text shown on the results page and to save searches for future reference. There are some "newer" search engines that have more of a visual approach to searching, such as KartOO and Ask.

The search engine Google initially launched in 1998 and quickly became so popular that the word "google" itself became synonymous with searching for information online. It is now the largest and most popular search engine. Google ranks Web sites by popularity, basing its rankings on what other pages link or refer to it and tends to find pages that other users have visited recently.

Google was founded in 1998 by Larry Page and Sergey Brin. The company's search engine is now one of the best known and most far-reaching in the world.

Today, Google is far more than a search engine. It now offers a highly developed mapping system, allows users to share their documents online, and even allows users to search inside books that have been electronically scanned into a database. While other search engines may offer some of these features, none is currently as comprehensive as Google.

The Query Process

The query process that search engines use is the final and most complex part of the search engine. For search engine users, the query process is fairly simple. Users type their search terms into a part of the search engine's Web page called a field and click on a button to see results. Today's search engines work extremely quickly, seldom giving users time to wonder how they gather information before displaying a page of results ranked by how relevant they are to the search terms.

In the seconds it takes for a search engine to return results, the search engine is evaluating all of the Web pages in its database using all kinds of different factors and sets of mathematical rules called algorithms to figure out what pages are relevant. The exact process varies among search engines, and search engine companies closely guard the algorithms they use to figure out what pages are relevant and rank the results.

Though the algorithms are considered trade secrets by search engine companies, most search engines still follow a few general rules. One key ranking rule is the placement of keywords and the frequency with which they appear on a Web page. Search engines will consider Web pages with the search terms in the heading, or "title tag," at the top of the screen to be more relevant to the search terms than other pages. The same is true of Web pages in which the search terms appear frequently. The search engine assumes that these Web pages are more relevant than other pages. Some search engines even develop preprogrammed results for common search phrases, such as movie titles.

TEN GREAT QUESTIONS

TO ASK AN INFORMATION SPECIALIST

1 How do I search for public documents online?

2 How do I decide what Web sites are relevant to my topic?

3 How many Web pages do I have to look at before I find what I'm looking for?

4 How do I decide whether or not I can trust a site?

5 What kinds of sites have the best information for my topic?

6 How do I come up with good search terms?

7 Are there any search engine shortcuts I can use to find information?

8 How do I use the advanced search options on a search engine's Web page?

9 When do I know that I have enough information?

10 What Web resources are available for helping me refine my search?

Chapter 2

Starting Out with Word Searches

All search engines use keyword searches typed in by the user to find information. The simplest search consists of typing a single word into the search field and seeing results. However, unless the word is very specific, the user is likely to be overwhelmed by a flood of information. For example, typing the word "pirate" into the Google search field will net more than seventy-five million results. Some link to biographies of famous pirates, while other results range from references to copyright violations to games to sports teams that use pirates as their mascots.

To avoid creating this kind of situation, users should first have a good idea of exactly what kind of information they want to find. This will allow the user to come up with good search terms. Since "pirate" is far too broad a search term, the searcher may want to add other key words to the search.

As the search becomes more specific, results will also become more refined. Typing "pirate captain" into the search field narrows the search to more than one million, and more of those results will focus on information about pirates. Typing in "pirate captain Blackbeard" brings the number

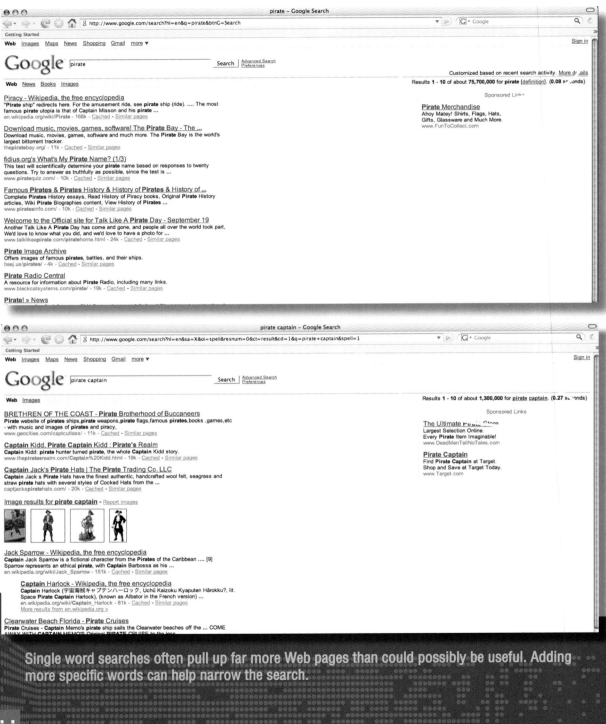

Single word searches often pull up far more Web pages than could possibly be useful. Adding more specific words can help narrow the search.

of results down to about twenty-three thousand, with many focusing on a particularly infamous pirate captain. If a user happens to know that the pirate Blackbeard died off the coast of North Carolina and adds that to the search terms, the search narrows to about six thousand.

Narrowing Results

Six thousand Web pages that mention the pirate Blackbeard are still far too many for a single person to read. Deciding which of these Web pages to look at can be tricky. While many of the Web pages listed in the results may contain accurate information from good sources, others may be incorrect, misleading, or completely irrelevant.

Most search engines today provide a few lines of text showing the context in which the search term was used, and users can often figure out whether or not a Web site will be useful from those lines of text. If the text is written in a language that the user can't read, it probably won't be very useful unless the search engine has a translation feature. It will also probably be obvious if the search term is being used in a work of fiction, a joke, or in a context that is completely opposite from what the user needs.

Of course, even the best information sometimes goes out of date as events transpire or more facts are uncovered. When dealing with the sciences, politics, current events, or any number of other topics, information can change daily or even hourly, and it is important to get the latest data. Fortunately, many Web sites linked with journals, magazines, and other publications sort their articles by date or even by time posted, offering the most recent items on the site's first page. Older articles are often stored in a database, which users can search. Some Web sites for individuals or organizations may not keep their information quite so fresh, though they may let the user know when the site was last updated.

Looking for a list of links to other Web sites can quickly expand the range of results from a word search. Usually, a links page will offer a brief description of the site so that users can decide if it will be relevant to them. Some of these links may offer information on topics that are closely related

Public Records Online

Public records often contain excellent raw information for research projects. These can range from Federal Bureau of Investigation (FBI) files on dead celebrities to local zoning laws. Today, many such documents can be found online by searching local, state, and federal government Web sites. Even if a local government doesn't have the documents posted, its Web site may tell you where to find them. For many federal and state government agencies, you can fill out a Freedom of Information Act request for the documents online. The Freedom of Information Act is a federal law guaranteeing a citizen's right to government information, and it allows citizens to request government documents. Remember that some government information—facts that may compromise national security or violate a citizen's privacy—are not subject to the law and that some information on documents may be blacked out by the agency and therefore be completely unreadable.

to the search terms. A Web site about the pirate Blackbeard, for example, may have a link to another site about life in coastal towns during the eighteenth century. Links like these can often help a user gain perspective on his or her topic.

Web Site Classifications

Generally, Web sites can be placed into six different categories: advocacy, business, informational, news, personal, and entertainment. Advocacy sites exist to influence public opinion or to promote a cause or a nonprofit organization. Business sites generally promote a product or service. Informational sites exist to provide factual information to the public. News sites offer information about local, regional, national, or international news. Personal sites usually offer information about an individual, such as his or her interests. Entertainment sites simply exist to entertain.

URLs and Domain Names

One way to determine if search results are helpful is to look at the URL for the Web pages that have been returned. Every Web site on the Internet has a URL, which enables Internet users to easily access Web sites that are hosted by different servers through the Web browser. Part of the URL contains the domain name, which consists of two parts. The first part of the domain name often identifies the organization, while the second part, called the generic top-level domain, tells the user what sort of organization it is.

There are five generic domain names currently in use in the United States: .gov, .com, .net, .edu, and .org, as well as several others that are not used as frequently. Some experts in Internet research rank the relevance of Web sites based on the domain name.

Sites tagged .edu and .k12 are often considered trustworthy because they are used for college and university sites. College and university Web pages may include a host of information from various academic departments, from the results of research projects to background information on famous alumni or even copies of documents owned by the school's library. Still, some college departments may be lax in updating the information on their sites. Also, students and even staff members may post incorrect information online.

Federal government departments use the .gov and .mil domain names. The many departments and bureaus using .gov range from the FBI to the Library of Congress. Web pages for government bureaus often contain raw data, such as census numbers, and a brief abstract explaining what the numbers mean. Congressional Web sites may have information about legislation under consideration or laws that have already been passed. Some government Web sites may also post information on how various government bureaus work or offer tips for the public. Many even offer a form for users

The federal government makes a wide array of information available online. The government's official search engine, USA.gov, provides directories to help users narrow their searches.

to request government documents using the Freedom of Information Act. Government Web sites are generally considered trustworthy and, for the most part, are complete, excluding national security information, though they are not always easy to navigate.

Web sites that use the other three domain names often require more scrutiny. Sites that use .org are often nonprofit organizations. These groups are usually committed to a specific agenda and are interested in sharing information about what they do. They can range widely from public library Web sites to nationwide conservation groups to local church groups. Some

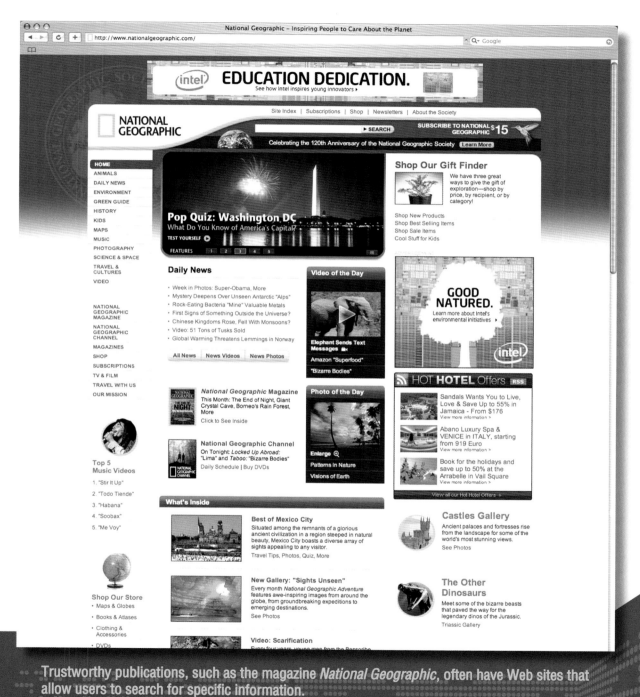

Trustworthy publications, such as the magazine *National Geographic*, often have Web sites that allow users to search for specific information.

of these sites may provide a great deal of accurate information, while others say very little. With these sites, it is often a good idea to double-check information against information found in other sources, as the information may be politically biased. Also look for contact information and a list of Web links on the Web site, both of which may provide information about the people running the site and the accuracy of their information.

Web sites using .com domains are commercial sites. The information on these sites may vary widely. Some may be very scholarly or the Web sites of reputable publications, such as the *New York Times* or *National Geographic* magazine. Others may contain incorrect information or even be deliberately inaccurate. Look for the names of reputable companies or known experts in the field, and study any links. Information on these sites should also be double-checked. The same is true for Web sites that use .net, which are usually Internet networks.

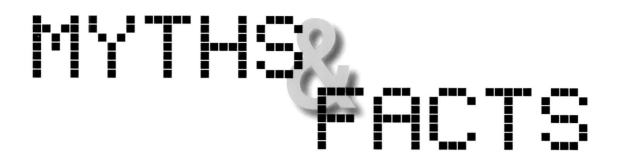

MYTH The Internet and the Web are the same thing.

FACT Though the Web allows access to millions of sites that use the same protocol to exchange information, it only represents a portion of the whole Internet.

MYTH All search engines are basically the same.

FACT Search engines operate differently, from how they sort information to how they present on the page.

MYTH The links near the top of the search engine's return page are always the best.

FACT Some search engines take money from companies to make sure their Web pages are listed at or near the top.

Chapter 3

Advanced Search Strategies

f a word search turns up too many or too few links, it may be time to go beyond word searches to refine the search. The user can look in online subject directories to find more specialized Web pages. Wildcards may help a user expand a search that at first seems to be going nowhere. And if there are too many results, there's always the option of changing the search terms to something more specific or trying a phrase search.

Phrase Searches

Phrase searches consist of a phrase placed inside double quotation marks. This tells the search engine to search for the exact phrase within the quotation marks. Instead of looking for search terms in any order, as they would with an ordinary word search, search engines take the terms placed in double quotes and search for them in that exact order.

Phrase searches often drastically reduce the number of returns by eliminating Web pages that do not have the terms in the exact order. They are particularly useful if a user is looking for a quote from a speech, the title of a book, or a full name. Phrase searches also can be used alongside ordinary word searches to help focus a search or alongside other phrases.

While phrase searches can sometimes help a user find specific information more quickly, there are pitfalls. Spelling can sometimes be a problem with phrase searches, as the smallest typing mistake when entering search terms can prevent a user from seeing helpful sites. Phrase searches may help to narrow the list of returns, but in some cases, they may also prevent possibly useful sites from coming up.

Boolean Operators and Wildcards

Boolean operators are words that can be used to link search terms together to help narrow or broaden a search. The most common Boolean operators are the words "and," "or," and "not." These words are sometimes capitalized and are coded into the search engine's software to let the search engine know that it's supposed to perform a particular function when they are used. For example, using the search terms "camera AND instructions" will narrow the search by telling the search engine that the user is looking for articles or Web pages using both terms. "Camera OR darkroom" broadens the search by telling the search engine to find sites that include either term. Using "camera NOT digital" weeds out pages that are irrelevant to the user by indicating that the search engine should leave out any sites that use the second word. Boolean operators also may be represented by symbols. The "+" sign indicates the word "AND," while the "-" sign indicates "NOT."

Symbols are also used in word stemming searches. In word stemming searches, the user types only part of a word and inserts a symbol—often called a wildcard—to represent the untyped part, often at the end of a word. The symbol tells the search engine to look for variations on a word, rather than just searching for the word itself. Often, the symbol used is "*", but some search engines may use other symbols, such as "$," "!," or "#." With the wildcard, a user could type "pirate*" to tell the search engine to look for pirate as well as "pirates," "pirated," and "piratical." Wildcards

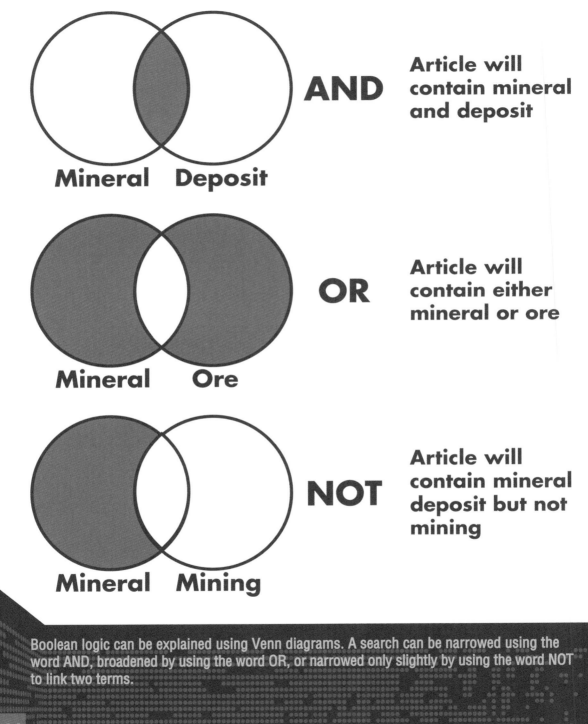

AND — Article will contain mineral and deposit

Mineral Deposit

OR — Article will contain either mineral or ore

Mineral Ore

NOT — Article will contain mineral deposit but not mining

Mineral Mining

Boolean logic can be explained using Venn diagrams. A search can be narrowed using the word AND, broadened by using the word OR, or narrowed only slightly by using the word NOT to link two terms.

therefore let users broaden their searches without having to type in all of the words they wanted to find.

The wildcard feature has to be specially designed into the search engine, a costly process. While many search engines that were started in the 1990s had this feature at one point, many have dropped it. However, wildcards are not entirely a thing of the past. The advanced search option on the search engine Google allows users to search using wildcards, and the function is used by many online resources, such as dictionaries and databases.

Advanced Searches

Most search engines have built-in features to let users expand or narrow their searches. Users can often reach these by clicking on an "advanced search" link on the search engine's Web site. Advanced search pages often have separate fields for exact phrase searches. Other fields let users enter combinations of search terms, broadening the search by looking for alternate words.

Advanced searches may also let users search for Web sites in other languages. While this may seem helpful only if a user can read the language, some major sites—such as those connected to governments or universities— offer translated versions through links on their pages. Also, the search engine AltaVista and some others have translation features that allow users to see a translated version of the Web page. Search engine translation features have limitations—translations may not cover all of the text on the page and are performed by computer programs, which can lead to imprecise word choices—but they can be useful if a user wants to see what an expert who speaks another language says or is interested in examining a topic from another culture's point of view.

Advanced search pages may have fields that allow users to type in words to exclude from the search. This feature can be helpful if a set of search terms keeps bringing up unwanted pages. For example, a user looking for Web sites about pirates may want to exclude the words "sports" or "ball" to direct the search away from sites about sports mascots.

Advanced search options can help users focus their search early on, allowing them to find pages they might have otherwise missed by using special features, such as AltaVista's translation service.

Some advance search options on search engines like Google are set up to allow users to look for a specific word within a specific URL.

Subject Directories

Subject directories are databases of Web sites and online documents organized by category, much like the Yellow Pages or business listings in a phone book. Just as a Yellow Pages user would look under the heading "restaurants"

File Edit View Favorites Tools Help

WIKIS AND BLOGS

Wikis and Blogs

Wiki sites and blogs have become very popular in recent years. Wikis are sites containing information represented as factual that allow users to log on and add content to Web pages or edit existing content. Blogs—or Weblogs— often function as online diaries, giving readers insight into the lives, thoughts, and opinions of their authors. Blogs began in the late 1990s and have become so mainstream that many news sites now have blog features written by journalists, and some independent blogs are considered trustworthy news sources. There are now specialized search tools designed just for searching blogs. Wikis began at about the same time as a way to let ordinary people share their knowledge on the Internet. One of the best-known wiki sites is Wikipedia, an online encyclopedia compiled through input from users. While both blogs and wiki sites may present factual information, users should be very careful about taking information from them unless it can be checked against other sources.

to find a pizza parlor nearby, subject directory users look under subject headings to find information on specific topics. They are usually incorporated within major search engines, but unlike search engines themselves, the categorization is performed by humans rather than computer programs. Results are returned in a series of menus arranged by subject. The search engine Yahoo! started out as a subject directory and still has an extensive subject directory. For example, users planning to visit a particular city can look that city up in the subject directory and then use it to find hotels, restaurants, museums, or other attractions.

CONDUCTING BASIC AND ADVANCED SEARCHES

Search engines try to rank the most relevant results first, while subject directories are organized in categories. These are usually presented alphabetically, and category titles may differ from one directory to the next. Subject directories take a great deal of effort to launch because people organize, evaluate, and catalog the information using predetermined criteria and then arrange, annotate, and code it. Therefore, their databases are usually much smaller than those of the search engines. They often make up for this by supplementing their results with results from search engine partners like Google or AltaVista.

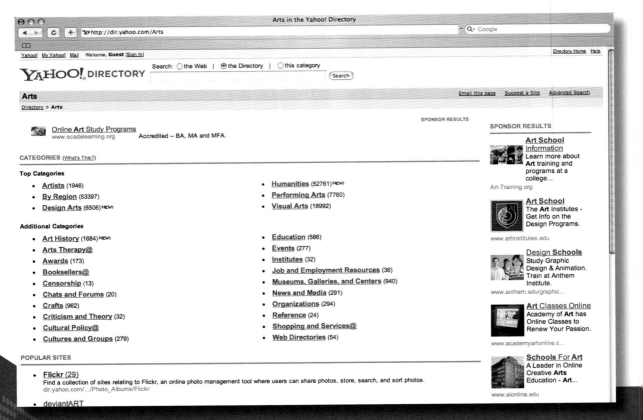

Directories help point researchers in a specific direction by presenting broad categories that can be narrowed until the user finds the information that he or she needs.

Subject directories can be great tools, particularly if a user is just getting started on a search. Users can use directory categories to help shape future searches, narrowing a general topic to more specific search terms. Results from subject directories are often very relevant to a general topic, since the pages in the directories are cataloged by people who evaluate them for their value to a topic.

However, there are also disadvantages. Since the subject directory databases are much smaller than those of search engines, users don't get as many returns on a search. Users also may not get the most up-to-date results possible when using subject directories. There can also be a significant time lag between the time that a page is published and the time it is entered into subject directories. While directory results are often highly relevant to search terms, many of the pages may be out of date—sometimes by years—even before they are evaluated and cataloged in the database.

Metasearch Engines

Metasearch engines are search engines that collect the results of other search engines. Essentially, this means that they search the indexes of multiple search engines at once. In other words, they plug your search terms into other search tools and bring back the results. On the surface, they work just like a regular search engine. A user types search terms into a field and clicks on a button telling it to find information. They extract what they interpret to be the most relevant results and returning those to the user. Popular metasearch engines include Dogpile, Clusty, and Beaucoup!.

Metasearch engines can be tremendous time savers because they can go through several search engines at once. They can be very helpful to users who are trying to get a general feel for what information is available online on a particular topic. They are also useful for finding a large number of results on a particular subject, searching the entire text of multiple documents, and for users with narrow or obscure research topics. Metasearch engines can also search the Web for particular types of documents, file types, source locations, or even for most recently updated documents.

However, obtaining results may take longer than with a regular search engine because they have to go through information from several databases. Metasearch engines may return incomplete results because they are denied access to some major search engines, such as Google. They may also dumb down search terms to speed the search process or search only a small

Metasearch engines retrieve information from multiple search engines at once. This can save users the trouble of typing search terms into multiple search engines.

portion of each search engine's database. Their results may also be somewhat skewed, as they often retrieve the first few links from each search engine, resulting in many links that come from sites that pay to have their links placed near the top of the results page. Of course, both subject directories and conventional search engines are also designed to make a profit and accept money to list certain Web sites closer to the top.

Chapter 4

Wrapping Up the Search

earch engines are often deceptively simple to use. Users may type in their terms, bring up a page of results, and simply use the first sites they click on as their sources of information without taking the time to evaluate them. On the other hand, some users may go through dozens of results looking for the perfect site without finding what they think they need.

Evaluating Web Sites

Chapter 2 touched on some quick and basic ways that a search engine user can quickly evaluate the usefulness of a Web site. However, even if the Web site appears to be useful on the surface, the user should still look deeper to evaluate the information that he or she receives. Users should look at the Web site and judge its accuracy, authority, objectivity, coverage, and whether or not the information is timely. The timeliness of information is known as currency.

Information found on the Web can't always be trusted. It is usually a good idea to cross-check information with other trusted sources.

File   Edit   View   Favorites   Tools   Help

JOURNALISM ON THE WEB

Journalism on the Web

In the early days of the Internet, few would have imagined that millions of people would someday read the news online. Many newspapers, television networks, and radio stations now post and update their stories online and are gradually moving toward creating original content for the Web only, responding to "nontraditional" news outlets that are based solely online. Journalism organizations have also responded to the growing trend over the years, posting tips for researching, writing, and developing content online, from how to post sound and video clips to how to remain current in the constant news cycle of today's world.

Many well-known newspapers, magazines, and even broadcast news networks now have their own Web pages that allow users to search for specific stories and information.

Accuracy

Often, the fastest way to confirm accuracy is to check the information against other sources. If the information on a Web site contradicts other current sources, there's a good chance that it's incorrect. Users should always be careful to check information found on the Internet against other sources, such as posted links to other pages and articles and, if possible, sources that are not online, such as authoritative books.

   Also check for grammatical errors and spelling mistakes. Even if a site originates from a trusted source, the information may not have been double-checked for accuracy before being posted online. If the Web page offers a research document or the results of a study, look for an explanation of how the data was collected and interpreted. If there is any doubt that the information on a Web page is inaccurate, the user should leave it out.

   It is also important to remember that just because several Web sites have the same information, that information could still be inaccurate. Many Web pages "mirror" information from other pages, meaning that they simply post the same information without checking it thoroughly for accuracy. This sometimes leads to the spread of inaccurate information and increases the importance of using other sources, such as books, to cross-check information. For example, a Google search for "Burmese mountain dog" will return about 289,000 hits, even though the breed's name is actually spelled "Burnese mountain dog."

Authority

Always look for information about a Web page's author or sponsor to help judge whether or not the information can be trusted. While anyone may write about a topic, it's always best to use information from people with certified qualifications. Look on the site for references to other publications from the page's author, as well as background information like work experience in the field, degrees, and affiliations with respected organizations. If the site does not list the people responsible for the information presented, check to see if the site was sponsored by an authoritative organization or entity.

Objectivity

Authors always have personal points of view. How much they allow their own feelings or beliefs to show may help a user decide whether or not their Web pages are useful. Journalists often try to present both sides of a story, and academic writers use arguments that cite the work of other scholars. Look for sites that present two sides of an argument or story. These perspectives show that the author did enough research to show a basic understanding of a topic's many facets.

Avoid information from controversial authors who may not present both sides or who don't cite their sources. These may be opinion pieces, and while the information within may be factual, there are likely to be many other sources that present the same information in a more scholarly way. However, there may be cases where it is necessary to use biased information in order to present both sides of the argument. In these cases, check the facts used in the pages, make it clear that the information is biased, and clarify what information might be inaccurate.

Coverage

Coverage deals with the amount of information presented on a Web site and how many details it covers. A Web site may be too general for the topic a user is researching or too detailed in aspects that are irrelevant to the search. Users should judge if a Web site presents specific information that fits the needs of their research or whether it is too broad or too narrow to use.

Currency

Currency refers to the timeliness of the information posted. As explained in chapter 2, users should check how often a site is updated or if the site

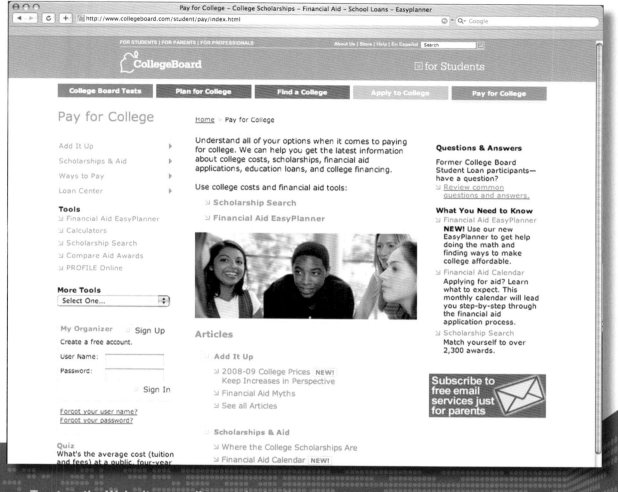

Trustworthy Web sites usually contain details about the person or organization posting the information, including contact information and links to other pages.

indicates when the last update was performed. While it may not matter how often a site is updated for some topics, for others, it is important to get the most up-to-date information. Some Web pages actually include dates showing the last time a page was updated.

Managing time wisely and staying focused are two of the easiest ways to help make sure that a Web search is successful.

Managing the Search

The size and sprawling nature of the Internet makes it possible to find information on nearly any subject. At the same time, it may also prove distracting. For some searches, hundreds or thousands of Web pages may be returned. While it's important to try to be thorough when doing research, it's also important to avoid getting bogged down in sites that may not be relevant.

One way users can avoid this is to have a clear idea of exactly what kind of information they need. Be as specific as possible with search terms to ensure that the pages most relevant to a topic are returned. If using multiple search engines, be sure to avoid visiting links that you've already seen. Also, remain focused on your goal. Search engines sometimes turn up irrelevant results. While some of these may be interesting, there's no point in spending a lot of time looking at them if they don't say anything about the search topic.

Since many search engines list links by their relevance, it is usually not necessary—and sometimes not possible—to go through all of them. Typically, returns become less relevant to the search terms used as you go down the list. To save time, you may want to concentrate on just the first few pages of returns. If there is nothing useful in the first few pages, it may be necessary to change the search terms.

It's also a good idea to limit search sessions to a certain time frame. Search for a while, and then do something else before returning to the search. Looking at Web pages can be tiring, and taking breaks from the search will help keep your mind fresh for evaluating Web pages.

GLOSSARY

algorithm A step-by-step process for solving a problem or finishing a task.

blog A shared online journal used by people to post their insights and information about their lives, interests, and experiences.

Boolean Relating to a mathematical system of notation invented in the nineteenth century that symbolically shows relationships between things and that has been applied to the Web by using the words "and," "not," and "or" to narrow or broaden searches.

browser A software program used to access the Internet in order to view documents.

catalog A complete list of items or information, usually arranged systematically.

category A collection of things that share something in common, as in topics in subject directories.

database An organized body of related information.

directory A listing of stored information.

domain name The part of a URL (Web address) that usually specifies the organization and type of organization and where a Web page is located.

Freedom of Information Act A law stating that every executive-branch government agency must publish instructions on how the public can get information from the agency.

Internet A worldwide network of computer networks that all use the same protocols to exchange data.

link An instruction that connects one part of a program or an element on a list to another program or list.

metasearch engines Search services that search several individual search engines at once and then combine the results.

network A system of interconnected computers that exchange data.

program A sequence of instructions that a computer can interpret and execute.

relevance The degree to which Web sites found are judged to be useful.

search engine A software tool that allows Web users to find information on the network.

server A computer that provides clients with access to files and printers as part of a shared network.

software Written programs or procedures or rules relating to the operation of a computer system.

subject directory Collections of high-quality Web pages organized into subject categories by people, often librarians or subject specialists.

URL Acronym for uniform resource locator, the address by which a Web page can be located on the Web.

Internet Society
1775 Wiehle Avenue
Suite 201
Reston, VA 20190-5108
(703) 439-2120
E-mail: isoc@isoc.org
Web site: http://www.isoc.org
The Internet Society was founded in 1992 to provide leadership in Internet
    related standards, education, and policy around the world.

Media Awareness Network
1500 Merivale Road, 3rd Floor
Ottawa, ON K2E 6Z5
Canada
(613) 224-7721
E-mail: info@media-awareness.ca
Web site: http://www.webawareness.org/english/index.cfm
This organization offers resources and support for anyone interested in media
    and information literacy for young people.

People for Internet Responsibility
PFIR c/o Peter G. Neumann
Principal Scientist
Computer Science Lab
SRI International EL-243
333 Ravenswood Avenue
Menlo Park, CA 94025-3493
(650) 859-2375

E-mail: neumann@pfir.org
Web site: http://www.pfir.org
This is a global, grassroots, ad hoc network of individuals who are concerned
about current and future operations, development, management, and
regulation of the Internet.

U.S. Internet Service Provider Association
700 12th Street NW
Suite 700E
Washington, DC 20005
(202) 904 2351
E-mail: kdean@usispa.org
Web site: http://www.usispa.org
The U.S. Internet Service Provider Association is a group representing the
interests of affiliated Internet service providers.

Web Sites

Due to the changing nature of Internet links, Rosen Publishing has developed
an online list of Web sites related to the subject of this book. This site is
updated regularly. Please use this link to access the list:

http://www.rosenlinks.com/dil/cbas

FOR FURTHER READING

Bingham, Jane. *Internet Freedom: Where Is the Limit?* Portsmouth, NH: Heinemann Library, 2006.

Gordon, Sherri. *Downloading Copyrighted Stuff from the Internet: Stealing or Fair Use?* Berkley Heights, NJ: Enslow Publishers, 2005.

Hawthorn, Kate. *The Young Person's Guide to the Internet.* New York, NY: Routledge, 2005.

Newman, Matthew. *You Have Mail: True Stories of Cybercrime.* London, England: Franklin Watts, 2007.

Parks, Peggy. *The Internet.* San Diego, CA: Lucent Books, 2005.

Souter, Gerry, Janet Souter, and Allison Souter. *Researching on the Internet Using Search Engines, Bulletin Boards, and Listservs.* Berkeley Heights, NJ: Enslow Publishers, 2003.

Torr, James. *Opposing Viewpoints: The Internet.* San Diego, CA: Greenhaven Press, 2005.

Witten, Ian, Marco Gori, and Teresa Numerico. *Web Dragons: Inside the Myths of Search Engine Technology.* San Francisco, CA: Morgan Kaufmann, 2006.

Ackerman, Earnest, and Karen Hartman. *The Information Searcher's Guide to Searching and Researching on the Internet*. Wilsonville, OR: ABF Content, 2001.

Baylin, Ed. *Effective Internet Search*. Ottawa, Canada: Baylin Systems, Inc., 2005.

Calishain, Tara. *Information Trapping: Real-Time Research on the Web*. Berkeley, CA: New Riders, 2007.

Diaz, Karen, and Nancy O'Hanlon. *IssueWeb: A Guide and Sourcebook for Researching Controversial Issues on the Web*. Westport, CT: Greenwood Publishing Group, Inc., 2004.

Hock, Randolph. *The Extreme Searcher's Internet Handbook*. Medford, NJ: CyberAge Books, 2004.

Kraynak, Joe. *Best of the Internet*. Indianapolis, IN: Que Publishing, 2005.

Milstein, Sarah, J. D. Biersdorfer, and Matthew MacDonald. *Google: The Missing Manual*. Cambridge, MA: O'Reilly Media, 2006.

Mintz, Anna, ed. *Web of Deception: Misinformation on the Internet*. Medford, NJ; CyberAge Books, 2002.

Radford, Marie, Susan Barnes, and Linda Barr. *Web Research: Selecting, Evaluating, and Citing*. New York, NY: Pearson Education, Inc., 2006.

Schlein, Alan. *Find It Online: The Complete Guide to Online Research*. Tempe, AZ: Facts on Demand Press, 2003.

INDEX

About the Author

Jason Porterfield has written more than twenty books for Rosen Publishing on subjects ranging from American history to environmental science.

Photo Credits

Cover, p. 1 (left) Romeo Gacad/AFP/Getty Images; cover, p. 1 (second from right), p. 38 Shutterstock.com; p. 7 © 2007 HowStuffWorks; p. 10 Michael Nagle/Getty Images; p. 33 © Rick Gomez/Corbis.

Designer: Nicole Russo; Editor: Nicholas Croce;
Photo Researcher: Cindy Reiman